Would You Rather

Book for Kids

A Hilariously Fun Activity Book

for the Entire Family

How to Play

Step 1

Split into two teams whether that be boys vs girls, kids vs parents, or any mix of your choice. If possible, also assign one person as a referee.

Step 2

Decide who gets to go first. Which team can do the most pushups? Which team can guess the number between 1 and 10 from someone not playing the game? Or just some good old fashioned rock paper scissors?

Step 3

The starting team has to ask a question from the book and the opposing team has 10 seconds to not only choose an option but to also give a meaningful reason as to why they chose what they did. The referee decides whether the answer is acceptable.

Step 4

The team can discuss their answer together but only one player can give the answer. The person answering has to alternate every turn.

Step 5

If the player who is answering can't choose or give a good reason then that player is out for the game and can't answer anymore or be involved in the team discussion.

Step 6

Repeat until all players are eliminated.

Would you rather...

*Be a superhero **OR** a wizard?*

Would you rather...

*Have the ability to fly **OR** read minds?*

Would you rather...

Lick the floor **OR** lick someone's armpit?

Would you rather...

Be a cat **OR** a dog?

Would you rather...

*Fall into a puddle of mud **OR** into a*

pile of yellow snow?

Would you rather...

*Do 100 pushups **OR** 100 situps?*

Would you rather...
*Get yelled at by Mom **OR** Dad?*

Would you rather...
*Run 10 miles **OR** bike 50 miles?*

Would you rather...

*Be a famous actor **OR** a famous athlete?*

Would you rather...

*Only be awake at night **OR** during the day?*

Would you rather...

Eat pizza for the rest of your life **OR** *burgers?*

Would you rather...

Only be able to eat breakfast **OR** *dinner forever?*

Would you rather...

Be a master at piano **OR** violin?

Would you rather...

Have a runny nose **OR** a stuffy nose?

Would you rather...

Never have to do homework again
***OR** be paid to do your homework?*

Would you rather...

*Be really cold **OR** really hot?*

Would you rather...

*Have only your legs **OR** only your arms?*

Would you rather...

*Be stranded in the desert **OR** in the rainforest?*

Would you rather...

Have the ability to speak any language **OR** play any instrument?

Would you rather...

Be super fast **OR** super strong?

Would you rather...

Stay up very late **OR** wake up very early?

Would you rather...

Never have to do homework again **OR** never take a test again?

Would you rather...

*Be stung by a bee once **OR** bitten by a mosquito ten times?*

Would you rather...

*Have a dinosaur **OR** a dragon as a pet?*

Would you rather...

*Be very fit and dumb **OR** very smart and skinny?*

Would you rather...

*Travel back in time **OR** to the future?*

Would you rather...

*Be the villain **OR** the hero in a movie?*

Would you rather...

*Be a famous singer **OR** a famous dancer?*

Would you rather...

Be 4'0 **OR** 8'0?

Would you rather...

Be in constant pain **OR** have a constant itch?

Would you rather...

Be covered in fur or scales?

Would you rather...

Use eyedrops made of lemon juice **OR** toilet paper made of sandpaper?

Would you rather...

Take a guaranteed $100,000 **OR** take a 50/50 chance at $500,000?

Would you rather...

Never be able to take a hot shower again **OR** never eat hot food again?

Would you rather...

*Never play **OR** always play and never win?*

Would you rather...

*Be deaf **OR** mute?*

Would you rather...

*Be a chronic farter **OR** a chronic burper?*

Would you rather...

*Only be able to shout **OR** whisper?*

Would you rather...

Never use an electronic device ever again **OR** never talk to a human again?

Would you rather...

Be a vegetarian **OR** only be able to eat meat?

Would you rather...

*Have 2 wishes today **OR** 3 wishes in 10 years?*

Would you rather...

*Go to a big party **OR** a small get together?*

Would you rather...

*Eat a stick of butter **OR** a teaspoon of cinnamon?*

Would you rather...

*Have to wear formal clothes for the rest of your life **OR** informal ones?*

Would you rather...

*Be hairless **OR** super hairy?*

Would you rather...

*Have to drink any liquid from a baby bottle **OR** have to always wear a diaper?*

Would you rather...

*Lick the floor **OR** lick someone's armpit?*

Would you rather...

*Always talk in riddles **OR** sing whenever you speak?*

Would you rather...

*Wear clown makeup for 6 months straight **OR** a pink tutu?*

Would you rather...

*Always have a booger showing in your nose **OR** food stuck in your teeth?*

Would you rather...

Eat cookies **OR** cake?

Would you rather...

Be the most popular kid in school **OR** the smartest?

Would you rather...

*Play inside all day **OR** outside?*

Would you rather...

Have to set the table before dinner
***OR** clean up after?*

Would you rather...

Live in Narnia **OR** in Hogwarts?

Would you rather...

Not use your phone **OR** computer for a month?

Would you rather...

Have the ability to become invisible

OR *fly?*

Would you rather...

Have only 3 close friends **OR** *many acquaintances?*

Would you rather...

*Be forced to listen to music all the time **OR** never listen to it?*

Would you rather...

*Live in **1900 OR 2100**?*

Would you rather...

Have the lights in your house always

*be on **OR** off?*

Would you rather...

Have to take ice cold showers for 20

*minutes each time to be clean **OR***

never be clean?

Would you rather...

*Be the best player on the losing team **OR** the worst player on the winning team?*

Would you rather...

*Be a genius in a world of idiots **OR** an idiot in a world of geniuses?*

Would you rather...

Accidentally pee your pants in public **OR** not brush your teeth for a week?

Would you rather...

Never wear shoes again **OR** never eat your favorite food again?

Would you rather...

*Have your clothes be **2** sizes too small **OR** 2 sizes too big?*

Would you rather...

*Not be able to taste **OR** smell?*

Enjoying the book so far? Let us know what you think by leaving a review!

What has been your favorite question from the book thus far?

Would you rather...

Have uncontrollable sneezing **OR** *uncontrollable farting?*

Would you rather...

Have the ability to freeze time **OR** *travel in time?*

Would you rather...

Not be able to listen to music **OR** *not watch TV?*

Would you rather...

Fight a bear **OR** *a lion?*

Would you rather...

*Find your true love **OR** have your dream job?*

Would you rather...

*Be trapped in a room with 100 spiders **OR** eat 3 spiders?*

Would you rather...

*Lose all your teeth **OR** your hair?*

Would you rather...

*Have all your clothes be bright lime green **OR** bright orange?*

Would you rather...

*Vacation in the mountains **OR** on the beach?*

Would you rather...

*Choose to play chess **OR** checkers?*

Would you rather...

Have to always wear jeans when you go out of the house **OR** *never again?*

Would you rather...

Invent a new gadget **OR** *discover a new scientific theory?*

Would you rather...

Have to change your job every year
OR *keep the same job for your*
whole life?

Would you rather...

Spend a day with you favorite fictional
character **OR** *favorite celebrity?*

Would you rather...

*Eat rotten eggs **OR** drink rotten milk?*

Would you rather...

*Eat raw meat **OR** moldy vegetables?*

Would you rather...

*Walk on hot coals for 10 seconds **OR** put your hands on a hot iron for 10 seconds?*

Would you rather...

*Have a couple small rocks in your shoes **OR** a bunch of mud?*

Would you rather...

*Be a world famous scientist **OR** artist?*

Would you rather...

*Be able to eat as much junk food as you want and not get fat **OR** receive a million dollars?*

Would you rather...

*Be able to see your own future **OR** other people's futures and not yours?*

Would you rather...

*Never remember faces **OR** names?*

Would you rather...

*Marry someone you don't love **OR** marry someone that doesn't love you?*

Would you rather...

*Have a unibrow **OR** a hairy back?*

Would you rather...

*Be a parent **OR** a child?*

Would you rather...

*Eat healthy everyday **OR** exercise everyday?*

Would you rather...

*Give up the internet for a month **OR***

transportation?

Would you rather...

*Be homeless **OR** have no friends?*

Would you rather...

*Look weak and be strong **OR** look strong and be weak?*

Would you rather...

*Not be able to ask questions **OR** give answers?*

Would you rather...

*Save someone you know **OR** 7 random people?*

Would you rather...

*Be rich and ugly **OR** poor and good looking?*

Would you rather...

Wear winter clothes in the Sahara **OR** *no clothes in the Arctic?*

Would you rather...

Lose $1000 **OR** *all of the contacts in your phone?*

Would you rather...

Give up pizza **OR** ice cream?

Would you rather...

Eat your own snot **OR** lick the bottom of your shoe?

Would you rather...

Be a lawyer **OR** a doctor?

Would you rather...

Be an astronaut **OR** sailor?

Would you rather...

*Have smelly feet **OR** bad breath?*

Would you rather...

*End all wars **OR** world hunger?*

Would you rather...

*Read a book **OR** watch a movie of the book?*

Would you rather...

*Be Batman **OR** Ironman?*

Would you rather...

Be Bruce Wayne **OR** Tony Stark?

Would you rather...

Live in Italy **OR** Greece?

Would you rather...

Live in Germany **OR** Switzerland?

Would you rather...

Learn Spanish **OR** Mandarin?

Would you rather...

Never have to pay for clothes again **OR** food?

Would you rather...

Go to the beach **OR** an amusement park?

Would you rather...

*Go to Disneyworld **OR** Universal Studios?*

Would you rather...

*Be able to talk with animals **OR** speak 7 languages?*

Would you rather...

*Win the lottery **OR** live an extra 12 years?*

Would you rather...

*Have super vision **OR** super hearing?*

Would you rather...

Have to make your own clothes **OR**
grow your own food?

Would you rather...

Have Rambo **OR** *the Terminator as*
your bodyguard?

Would you rather...

*Be gossiped about **OR** never talked about at all?*

Would you rather...

*Give up video games **OR** movies?*

Would you rather...

*Own a private jet **OR** 10 supercars and never have to pay for gas?*

Would you rather...

*Have free first class seats on a flight for life **OR** never pay for food?*

Would you rather...

*Have Christmas day be very cold but snowy **OR** sunny and warm?*

Would you rather...

*Have your feet be wheels **OR** your hands be knives?*

Would you rather...

Clean the floor with a toothbrush **OR**

mow the lawn with scissors?

Would you rather...

Make a small difference in 5 people's

lives **OR** *a big difference in 1 person's*

life?

Would you rather...

Have a rock chip in your shoe **OR** a hair in your eye?

Would you rather...

Drive a Mercedes Benz **OR** a BMW?

Would you rather...

*Drive a Toyota **OR** a Honda?*

Would you rather...

*Drive a Lamborghini **OR** Ferrari?*

Would you rather...

Have your sibling give you a wedgie **OR** throw dirt in your eye?

Would you rather...

Work at McDonalds **OR** Burger King?

Would you rather...

Work at Walmart *OR* McDonalds?

Would you rather...

Go to school *OR* work?

Would you rather...

Do a public dance **OR** speech?

Would you rather...

Celebrate Halloween **OR** Thanksgiving?

Would you rather...

Eat turkey on Thanksgiving **OR** candy on Halloween?

Would you rather...

Get a papercut every time you touched paper **OR** bite your tongue every time you ate food?

Would you rather...

Eat Indian food **OR** Mexican food?

Would you rather...

Be able to teleport **OR** read minds?

Would you rather...

*Wear your grandma's clothes **OR** have her hairstyle?*

Would you rather...

*Be able to control fire **OR** water?*

Would you rather...

*Be able to control water **OR** air?*

Would you rather...

*Be a mage **OR** a warrior?*

Would you rather...

*Always be 45 minutes early **OR** 10 minutes late?*

Would you rather...

*Solve global warming **OR** end world hunger?*

Would you rather...

*Go blind **OR** lose all your memory?*

Would you rather...

*Give up texting **OR** calling?*

Would you rather...

*Be able to tell if someone is lying **OR** always get away with a lie?*

Would you rather...

*Be famous **OR** powerful?*

Would you rather...

Have an oversized head **OR** a very high pitched voice?

Would you rather...

Sound like Jar-Jar Binks from Star Wars **OR** Siri?

Would you rather...

*Always be stuck in traffic **OR** always have slow internet?*

Would you rather...

*Have your breath come out as **Darth** Vader's **OR** your voice come out as Yoda's?*

Would you rather...

*Lose the ability to lie **OR** believe everything you hear to be true?*

Would you rather...

*Hear the good news **OR** bad news first?*

Thank you for reading! If you enjoyed the book, leave us a review and let us know what you liked or what you would like to see next.

As a special bonus, enjoy this exclusive preview of one our other popular titles!

Try Not To Laugh Challenge

Challenge

Summer Campfire Edition Joke Book

How To Play

Step 1

Split into two teams whether that be boys vs girls, kids vs parents, or any mix of your choice. If possible, also assign one person as a referee. You can also do 1 vs 1!

Step 2

Decide who gets to go first. Which team can do the most pushups? Which team can guess the number between 1 and 10 from someone not playing the game? Or just a good old fashioned game of rock paper scissors?

Step 3

The starting team has to tell a joke from the book. You can say the joke however you like and animate it too with funny faces, gestures, or whatever else.

Step 4

If everyone on the opposing team laughs, the other team gets a point! Set a limit for how many points it takes to win and the first team to reach the limit, wins!

What do you call a dear with no eyes?

(In a southern accent) I have no idear!

How does a pirate prefer to travel?

By ARRRRRR-V

What do you say to a one legged hitch hiker?

Hop in!

Why did the duck say bang?

Because he was a firequacker!

Why don't lobsters share?

They're shellfish.

What is brown and sticky?

A stick!

What do you get when you cross a dinosaur with fireworks?

Dinomite

What's tree plus tree?

Sticks

What do you call a guy with no arms and legs on the side of a mountain?

Cliff

What do you call a woman with no arms and legs on the beach?

Sandy

What did the mushroom say when he wasn't invited to the party?

But I'm such a fun-gi!

My brother and I were fighting each other yesterday...

It was in tents!

I asked Google how to start a campfire without tools...

It gave me 20 million matches!

I love campfire smoke so much...

It brings tears to my eyes.

Want to hear my campfire jokes?

They're straight fire!

I got a job as a human cannonball...

I was immediately fired.

What's the difference between a duck and George Washington?

One has a bill on his face while the other has his face on a bill!

Why didn't the Mexican archer fire his bow?

He didn't habanero!

I never go camping with only one other person...

It's just two in tents!

What do camping and fancy hotels have in common?

Toilet trees are complementary!

What do you get when you cross Captain America with the Incredible Hulk?

The Star Spangled Banner

What sound does a nut make when it sneezes?

Cashew!

I went to buy some camouflage trousers...

But I couldn't find any!

I've just come back from a once in a lifetime trip...

Never again!

What did the two fish in the tank say to each other?

How do you drive this thing??

What's orange and sounds like a parrot?

A carrot

I slept like a log last night...

I woke up in the campfire.

What was General Washington's favorite tree?

Infantry

What do you call cheese that isn't yours?

Nacho cheese

Why did the toilet paper roll down the hill?

To get to the bottom!

What do bears call campers in sleeping bags?

Soft tacos

Why did Humpty Dumpty like camping in autumn?

Because he had a great fall!

Did you hear about the camper who broke his left arm and leg?

He's all right now.

What do you call a camper without a nose OR body?

Nobody knows!

What do you get when you cross a fish and two elephants?

Swimming trunks

What do clouds do when they get rich?

They make it rain

How do trees access the internet?

They log in.

What do you call a bear with no teeth?

A gummy bear

How do you catch a squirrel?

Climb a tree and act nutty!

Why is a river rich?

Because it has two banks.

If you enjoyed this title, check out our other books by searching "Hayden Fox" on Amazon!